Gift from:

I0079342

Name:

Address:

Email:

Misc.

"Surviving Smart: A Teen's Guide to Navigating Parents and Guardians"

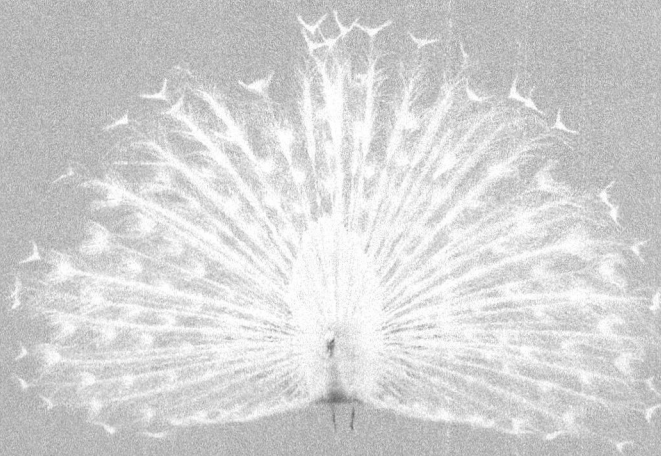

Published by My Littl' Workshop
For permissions or inquiries, contact the author Rev. Dr. Brevil or the publisher My Littl' Workshop

Cover art by Artist/Designer Prince Jai & MLW
Interior design © Marie S. Brevil/ MLW

This book is a work of non-fiction intended to inspire and empower. The author and publisher disclaim any liability for any direct or indirect loss or damage resulting from the use of this book.

Printed in the United States of America.

Marie S. Brevil

Surviving Smart

"A Teen's Guide to Navigating Parents and Guardians"

Marie Brevil

Preface

Every journey begins with a single step — and often, that step takes courage, especially when you're walking a path that no one else can fully see or understand.

This book is a gift to you — the teen who feels unseen, unheard, or misunderstood. It's a guide to help you navigate the twists and turns of family life, especially when things get complicated or tough. But more than that, it's a call to remember your power, your worth, and your light.

You are not alone. You have within you a strength that can break cycles, heal wounds, and build a future that honors your true self. This journey won't always be easy, but it will be worth it.

I invite you to walk with me, to listen deeply to your heart, and to claim your space unapologetically. This is your time. This is your story. Let's begin.

Dedication

This book is dedicated to my wonderful teen — my greatest supporter, my relentless challenger, my teacher, and my inspiration. You keep me grounded, focused, and honest. You push me to be better, to speak clearer, and to stay on the right path, even when it's hard to see. Your ideas and energy are a force to be reckoned with, and I am so proud to be chosen to walk this journey with you.

To every teen who opens this book: may you find strength in these pages. May the wisdom here help you rise, heal, and build a life full of joy and power. Your story matters, and your light is needed in this world.

To every caring parent who chooses this book for their teen: thank you for proving that love is action. Family, parenting, and raising children is a continuous journey — a team effort built on love, communication, and respect. Remember, to care for others well, you must also care for yourself first. Together, we rise.

Welcome, we want you to know that's a powerful and important book you're about to read. Teens often feel powerless around their parents, and other adults, especially when the home environment is difficult or toxic. A guide like this could equip you with practical strategies, emotional wisdom, and the tools to thrive despite those challenges.

Buckle up! This is going to be fun.

4. Becoming a Person of Value: How to Make Yourself Needed (Without Selling Out)

- Ways to build value in your household and community
- How to offer help that's actually appreciated, not annoying
- Building your reputation quietly and steadily

5. The Power of Charisma and Emotional Intelligence

- What charisma really means for teens
- Simple ways to build connection, trust, and respect
- How charisma can be your shield and your key

6. Protecting Your Mental and Emotional Health

- Setting invisible boundaries with toxic parents
- Finding safe spaces and people to talk to
- Techniques for staying calm and centered during conflict

7. Black Sheep and Beyond: How to Shine When You're Ignored or Blamed

- Why being "the black sheep" can be your secret power

- Stories and examples of teens who thrived despite rejection
- Cultivating resilience and self-love

8. How to Get Help When You Need It
- Trusted adults, counselors, hotlines, and resources
- When and how to ask for help without fear
- Planning for independence and your future

9. Conclusion: Your Life Is Bigger Than Your Home
- Encouragement for the journey ahead
- Affirmations for self-worth and growth
- Call to action: Start building your life your way

10. Start Building Your Empire Now — While You Still Can

11. Count on Nobody but Yourself — Your Ultimate Power

Bonus Chapter: Save Yourself

We want you to know that, there is no need to feel intimidated, we keep the tone real, empowering, and practical for you because you are special, important, and the most important player, you're the GOAT, now breathe.

Know that those are powerful themes created for you, so you know and stay aware of how imperative it is to keep building your future early while you still have freedom, and cultivating total self-reliance so you're never left feeling betrayed or let down.

If you ever feel overwhelmed, put the book down, drink some water, breathe, meditate, or start a loving, and peaceful conversation with your parent, or a close friend regarding the topic that made you feel overwhelmed.

You may also invest some time with your own self to reflect and comprehend why are you feeling the way you do, is it attachment, fear to let go, or what is at the root of those feelings.

This book is a guide to help you build strength,

power, respect, and confidence without shame, while also preparing for a better future.

Reminder:

Start Building Your Empire Now — While You Still Can

You might think building your future is something you do after school, after college, or after life gets "serious." But here's a truth that most grown-ups forget to tell you: The best time to start is now. While you still have the freedom to explore, dream, and even make mistakes without major responsibilities, you have a golden opportunity to plant seeds for your empire.

What does building your empire mean?
It's not just about money or fame. It's about creating your own foundation — your skills, your confidence, your network, and your mindset — so when life throws challenges your way, you're ready. It's about owning your story and crafting the life you want on your own terms.

You don't have to have everything figured out. You don't have to wait for someone to hand you permission or resources. Use your time now to:

- Discover your talents and interests
- Learn new skills — even online for free
- Build relationships with people who lift you up
- Save small amounts of money, even if it's just a little
- Practice discipline and habits that support your goals

And yes — have fun with your friends, laugh, make memories. That's part of your foundation too. You don't need to sacrifice your joy to build your empire. In fact, joy and connection are your fuel.

Remember: Your empire starts with you, right where you are.

No worries, I will remind you again later:

Count on Nobody but Yourself — Your Ultimate Power

This might sound harsh, but it's one of the most important truths to know: People can disappoint you. Sometimes they don't mean to. Sometimes they don't even realize it. But sometimes, they just won't come through — no matter how much you hope.

That doesn't mean everyone will betray you, but it means you have to be prepared just in case. The key to staying strong and unshakable is this: Count on yourself first and always.

When you rely on yourself, no one can let you down. You become your own protector, your own provider, your own greatest champion. You take full responsibility for your life — and that means you get to choose how you respond, what you build, and who you allow in.

This doesn't mean you don't trust or love others. It

means you put yourself first in a way that keeps you safe and empowered.

Here's how to start:

- Make promises to yourself and keep them
- Develop habits that build your strength and confidence
- Learn to solve problems on your own, then ask for help when needed — but never depend fully on anyone else
- Practice saying "no" to things and people who don't serve you
- Celebrate your wins, no matter how small

You are the foundation of your future. When you stand firm on yourself, nothing or no one can shake your peace or your power.

Bonus Chapter: Save Yourself

This chapter is one of the most important messages you'll ever get — because your life, your future, and your spirit depend on it. (So this is a foretaste of what awaits you).

First, as a child or teen in this case, or even if you were a young adult, DO NOT rush to have a child.

Enjoy your youth. Explore, learn, and make mistakes, but don't let anyone pressure you to give away your power before you're ready. Every time you lie down with someone, you are sharing their energy, their karma, their family story — whether you realize it or not. What if the person's family has a history of pain, violence, or curses? Without your willing knowledge, you could be carrying burdens that aren't yours. Stay wise. Protect your energy. Never let adults touch you in ways that feel wrong or uncomfortable.

This is manipulation. They are stealing your energy and stealing your light. This kind of harm sticks around longer than you think — even if you learn how to heal later.

You don't have to curse those adults, but if they violate you, you have every right to protect yourself spiritually and physically. Pray for trustworthy adults to guide you, but trust yourself first. Your gut is your guardian — if it says run, then run.

Respect your parents no matter what.
You don't have to agree with everything they say or do, but don't disrespect, shame, humiliate, or curse them. They hold a sacred connection to you — your umbilical cord, your life, your ancestral lineage. That connection carries spiritual weight. We won't get too deep here, but it's enough to say: guard your words and actions toward them, even if the relationship is hard.

Don't get involved with married people.
This might sound like old-fashioned advice, but it's true — relationships with married people carry hidden curses. They come with complex karma and alliances you don't want. You become marked and blocked from blessings. They're a team that may turn against you later. Protect your peace and your future by choosing wisely.

Give yourself strong life principles to avoid traps. Negative forces want to trap you in cycles of pain, betrayal, and limitation. But you have power — more than you realize. Your ancestors are waiting on you to rise up, correct what's broken, protect your line, and break generational curses.

You are the one.
You have the strength, wisdom, and light to heal yourself and your family legacy. Honor that power. Save yourself — body, mind, and spirit.

Introduction:
Welcome to Your Power — This Book Is For YOU

Hey, you. Yes, you — the one who's reading this right now. Maybe life at home feels tough, unfair, or confusing. Maybe you feel invisible, blamed, or just tired of trying to fit in where it doesn't feel right.

I want you to know something important right here, right now: You are powerful beyond measure. Your story matters. Your future is yours to create. No matter what your parents, guardians, or anyone else says or does, you have the strength inside to rise, to heal, and to build the life you deserve.

This book isn't about blaming anyone — it's about YOU. It's about helping you survive smartly and grow powerfully. It's about learning how to protect yourself, set boundaries, build value, and shine — even when it feels like the world wants to dim your light.

There's no perfect way to do this. You won't get it all right the first time. But that's okay. This book is like a friend who's been through it and wants to share the real talk and real tools to help you navigate your journey.

Are you ready? Because your power is waiting.

How to Use This Book:
Your Guide to Growing Stronger Every Day

This book is made for you to use — not just to read. Here's how to get the most from it:

1. Take Your Time
Don't rush through. Each chapter has lessons, examples, and exercises designed to help you understand yourself better and build new skills. Read one chapter at a time. Reflect on it. Use the journal prompts and questions.

2. Be Honest with Yourself
The questions and journal entries are for YOU — no one else. Be real. Write what you really feel, think, and want. This is your safe space to explore.

3. Practice the Affirmations Daily
Affirmations are powerful reminders of your worth and strength. Say them out loud, write them down, or meditate on them. Let them sink deep into your mind and heart.

4. Use the Exercises to Build Habits
Try the practical exercises regularly. Whether it's setting boundaries, managing your emotions, or building your future, consistency will change your life.

5. Protect Your Energy
This book teaches you how to set boundaries and protect yourself — use these tools. Your peace is precious.

6. Return When You Need
Life changes. Challenges come and go. Come back to this book anytime you need guidance, encouragement, or a reminder of your power.

Your journey to freedom, strength, and self-love starts here. Let's go — you've got this.

Chapter 1:
You're Not Alone — Understanding Family Dynamics

Why Parents Act the Way They Do
Sometimes, parents aren't perfect. They come from their own family stories — things they learned growing up, past hurts, and sometimes just their ego getting in the way. Some parents are strict, some are distant, and some treat certain kids differently. It's not always fair, but it's often about them, not you.

The Unfairness of Favoritism and Invisible Kids
Have you noticed how some siblings or cousins get all the attention, while others feel invisible? Sometimes parents "pick favorites" — it can feel like they don't see or care about you the same way. That hurts. But it's not because you're less worthy. It's a problem with their own issues, not your value.

This Book Is About You — Your Survival and Growth
You might feel lost or angry sometimes because you don't have anyone guiding you through these family storms.

Think of this book as a friend who's been through similar stuff and wants to share what works. You don't have to agree with everything here, but at least now you have tools to make smarter choices.

Example
Imagine two siblings, Mia and Malik. Mia always gets praised and rewarded, but Malik feels ignored no matter what he does. Malik starts to think maybe he's the problem. But really, their parents are dealing with their own stresses and history — and it's not Malik's fault. Malik learns to find his own value outside of his parents' opinions.

Message
Your parents' actions don't define your worth. You are valuable, seen, and important — even when it feels like no one is watching.

Reflection
Think about your family. Have you noticed times when someone got more attention or love? How did it make you feel? Remember, it's not about you — it's about their own story.

Journal Entry

Write about a time you felt invisible or less important in your family. What did you wish could be different? What can you do now to remind yourself you are important?

Questions to Ask Yourself
- How do I feel when I'm ignored or treated unfairly?
- What are three things I like about myself that have nothing to do with my family?

Questions to Ask Your Parents (when safe)
- Can you tell me about your childhood and what was hard for you?
- How can we help each other understand each other better?

Principles to Build
- Your worth is NOT based on how others treat you.
- Everyone has a story that affects how they act.
- You have the power to create your own identity outside your family's drama.

Aha Moment

You realize that your parents are human too — with their own struggles — and their behavior is about them, not you. This understanding can help you stop blaming yourself and start focusing on your own growth.

Affirmations

- I am worthy of love and respect, no matter what.
- My value is not defined by how others treat me.
- I am growing stronger every day, independent of my family's past.
- I choose to focus on my own growth and happiness.
- I am seen, I am heard, and I matter.

Chapter 2:
Why Parents Stop Covering You (And What That Means)

What It Means When Parents Stop "Covering" You
When parents stop "covering" you, it means they're no longer shielding or protecting you — physically, emotionally, or spiritually. That protection can feel invisible but it's real. Without it, you might feel like you're out there alone when trouble comes. You may not have someone to stand up for you or help you when things get tough.

How That Affects You Emotionally and Practically
This can hurt in ways you don't even expect. You might feel abandoned, invisible, or unimportant. Sometimes, your parents or grandparents went through the same thing, and if the cycle isn't broken, it can keep repeating. So it's important to notice this and learn to ask yourself the right questions — like, what do I really need? How can I protect myself?

Understanding Their Limits and Patterns
Forgiveness is powerful, but it should never cost

your peace. Watch for patterns and set boundaries early. Don't let anyone — not even your parents — use your talents or gifts without your permission. If something makes you uncomfortable, speak up and be firm.

You've probably seen families where one kid is the "black sheep" — the one who gets blamed or used — while another is strong and doesn't let anyone walk over them. That strength comes from setting boundaries and focusing on yourself.

Be that kid. Demand respect from everyone — your friends, family, even your country's president. If they don't respect you, don't give them access to your presence. Let them feel your absence. You are special and important. Don't forget that.

Example
Jalen's parents stopped defending him after a big argument. Suddenly, he felt like he was on his own when trouble started at school. But instead of giving up, Jalen learned to protect himself by speaking up, setting boundaries, and focusing on what he could control.

Message
Even if your parents aren't protecting you, you can learn to protect yourself. Your peace and safety come first.

Reflection
Think about a time you felt like your parents weren't there to support you. How did that make you feel? What did you do to get through it?

Journal Entry
Write about the boundaries you want to set with the people in your life. What would you say if someone crossed those boundaries?

Questions to Ask Yourself
- What are my limits, and how can I protect them?
- When have I felt invisible or unprotected, and what did I learn?

Questions to Ask Your Parents (when safe)
- Can we talk about how you show love and protection?
- How can we work together so I feel safer and respected?

Principles to Build
- Forgiveness doesn't mean sacrificing your peace.
- Boundaries protect your energy and your future.
- Your talents and gifts are yours — protect them.
- Demand respect always; your presence is valuable.

Aha Moment
You realize that protecting yourself starts with setting clear boundaries and demanding respect — no matter who the other person is.

Affirmations
- I have the right to protect my energy and my boundaries.
- My peace is more important than anyone's approval.
- I am worthy of respect from everyone in my life.
- I choose to stand strong and guard my gifts.
- I am powerful even when others don't protect me.

Chapter 3:
Reading Your Parents' Patterns — When to Step Up and When to Step Back

How to Observe and Decode Your Parents' Moods and Behaviors

You've got to learn how to "read the room" — to notice when your parents are tired, stressed, or just not in the mood. If you walk in and they're already upset, don't ask for favors or money. Instead, show you care: make some tea, clean up your space, or help around the house. If your mom is single, don't let her carry everything alone. Pitch in with chores like taking out the trash, washing dishes, or doing laundry.

Being helpful doesn't mean you're responsible for your parents, but it shows you're a good human being who cares. And when they're struggling financially, avoid asking for things they can't afford — it can make them feel embarrassed or helpless, which adds stress they don't need. Sometimes parents hide their pain and depression just to protect you.

If you have younger siblings, step up and help them without waiting to be asked. If you see a mess, clean it up — you live here too! Don't be "just humankind" — be a kind human being.

Strategies to Avoid Triggering Negative Reactions
Before you ask for anything, check your "case record." Is your room clean? Are your chores done? If not, finish those first. Don't expect help or favors if you leave your space messy or responsibilities undone. Be smarter than smart.

How to Predict When You're "On Their Radar" — and How to Get Off It
If your parents come home stressed from work, they might be looking for any excuse to snap. Stay 10 steps ahead: keep your room clean, do your homework, practice your music or skills, and don't give them any reason to complain. Be impeccable in your actions.

Use your words wisely. Keep conversations respectful and clear, not dramatic or combative. Stand your ground calmly and confidently — you're smart, special, and kind. Don't let their bad mood pull you down. Everything is energy; choose to stick to the good vibes.

Also, respect your parents' language and culture. If they're immigrants or speak other languages, learn those languages too. It shows respect and helps you connect deeper — to them, to your family, and to your ancestors. Don't lose that opportunity; it's part of your power.

Example
Leila notices her mom comes home tired every day. Instead of asking for new clothes or outings, she cleans the kitchen and helps her little brother with homework. When she does need to talk, she waits for a calm moment and speaks kindly. Her mom starts to relax and appreciate her more.

Message
Understanding and respecting your parents' moods and limits helps you avoid conflicts and build better connections. You don't have to give up your needs — just be smart about when and how you ask.

Reflection

Think about a time when you asked your parents for something and it didn't go well. What was happening with them at the time? How could you have approached it differently?

Journal Entry

Write down your parents' usual moods or habits. When do they seem happiest? When are they stressed? How can you adjust your actions to match those times?

Questions to Ask Yourself
- How can I show respect for my parents' feelings and struggles?
- What chores or help can I offer without being asked?

Questions to Ask Your Parents (when safe)
- What's been stressing you lately?
- How can I help make things easier at home?

Principles to Build
- Being helpful shows strength, not weakness.
- Timing and respect matter when asking for things.

- Communication should be calm, clear, and kind.
- Language and culture are powerful tools for connection.

Aha Moment

You realize that paying attention to your parents' moods and needs helps you avoid trouble and creates space for better conversations.

Affirmations

- I am observant and understand the feelings of those around me.
- I choose my words and actions wisely to create peace.
- I am helpful, respectful, and strong.
- I honor my family's culture and language as part of who I am.
- I am smart enough to build bridges, not walls.

Chapter 3:
Reading Your Parents' Patterns — When to Step Up and When to Step Back

This chapter is important so let's review it again and let's learn something new.

Learn to Read the Room
One of the smartest things you can do is learn to read your parents' moods and behaviors. Pay attention to their patterns — when they're tired, stressed, or upset. For example, if you know they've had a bad day, don't go asking for money or permission to hang out. Instead, show kindness: make some tea, clean your room, or help with chores. Small acts can go a long way.

If your mom is single, don't leave all the housework to her. Help with dishes, laundry, sweeping, or taking out the trash. Being responsible doesn't mean you have to carry their burdens, but it shows you care and are growing into a good human being — not just a "humankind." (That means: be kind and human.)

Understand Their Struggles

If your family is facing money problems, don't ask for things you know they can't afford. It might embarrass or stress them, and they might even regret the pressure of supporting you — not because you're not worth it, but because they feel helpless. Sometimes parents hide their pain or depression just to protect you, so be patient and supportive as best you can.

If you have younger siblings, step up to help without waiting to be asked. Help with their homework, watch out for their needs, and take responsibility where you can. When you see a mess, clean it up — you live there too. Sharing the load is a sign of maturity and respect.

Avoid Triggering Negative Reactions

Before you ask for anything, do your homework—literally and figuratively. Is your room clean? Are your chores done? If not, finish those first. Don't ask for favors or money if you're leaving your space messy or responsibilities unfinished. Think of yourself as your own lawyer — prepare your case before you go to the "tribunal" (your parents).

Stay Ahead of Their Radar

Parents can come home stressed from work, sometimes frustrated with things they can't control. Sometimes, they might seem like they're waiting to catch you messing up. Be 10 steps ahead: keep your space clean, do your homework, practice your skills, and don't give them any reason to complain.

When you talk to them, use your words carefully. Be respectful, clear, and calm — don't turn conversations into fights or shouting matches. Stand your ground with kindness and confidence. Remember, you are smart, special, and kind. Your good energy can't be polluted by their negativity if you don't let it.

Honor Their Language and Culture

If your parents speak multiple languages or come from another country, learning their language shows respect and helps you connect deeper with your family and ancestors. It's not just about words — it's about honoring your roots. If you only speak one language, you're missing out on a powerful way to grow as a family and open doors for your future.

Example

Leila notices her mom comes home tired and stressed. Instead of asking for money or permission right away, Leila helps clean the kitchen and assists her younger brother with homework. When she needs to talk, she waits for a calm moment and speaks kindly. Her mom starts to relax and appreciate her more.

Message

Paying attention to your parents' moods and needs helps you avoid conflicts and builds stronger relationships. You don't have to give up your needs — just learn to ask at the right time and in the right way.

Reflection

Think about a time you asked your parents for something and it didn't go well. What was happening with them at the time? How might you approach it differently now?

Journal Entry

Write down your parents' usual moods or habits. When are they happiest? When are they stressed?

How can you adjust your actions to fit those times?

Questions to Ask Yourself
- How can I show respect for my parents' feelings and struggles?
- What chores or help can I offer without being asked?

Questions to Ask Your Parents (when safe)
- What's been stressing you lately?
- How can I help make things easier at home?

Principles to Build
- Small acts of kindness can change the atmosphere.
- Timing and respect matter when asking for things.
- Calm, clear communication is the key to being heard.
- Knowing your family's language and culture is a powerful tool.

Aha Moment
You realize that reading your parents' moods and showing respect for their struggles helps you avoid

unnecessary conflicts and creates space for better conversations.

Affirmations

- I am aware and considerate of others' feelings.
- I choose kindness and respect in my words and actions.
- I am responsible and helpful without losing myself.
- I honor my family's roots as part of my power.
- I am smart and strong enough to build peace at home.

Chapter 4:

Becoming a Person of Value — How to Make Yourself Needed (Without Selling Out)

You can be needed without overdoing it or dimming your light. Sometimes parents might focus on one child more because they need that child to fill a space in their own lives. They may work hard to support that child but ignore or overlook the others. It's not fair, but it happens. Your value isn't about who gets the most attention — it's about who shows up for themselves and others in a healthy way.

Ways to Build Value in Your Household and Community

Look for ways to help out — volunteer, support your family, or assist others — but always make sure your own cup is full first. Don't drain yourself trying to please everyone. That's an illusion that never satisfies. You have to care for yourself before you can truly care for others.

How to Offer Help That's Actually Appreciated, Not Annoying

Don't overdo it. Think before you act. Know your limits and boundaries. Don't just do things so people will like you. Your time, energy, and effort are valuable — whether you're helping with homework, chores, or anything else. If someone doesn't respect your investment, don't fall prey to manipulators.

Some parents can be very manipulative. They might gossip on the phone for hours but expect you to handle heavy responsibilities — like taking care of four younger siblings — that aren't really your job. If that happens, be honest with them about what you can and cannot do. Speak up if it feels too much, especially if you're feeling overwhelmed or having harmful thoughts. If your parents don't listen, find someone else you trust — an aunt, grandma, teacher, or counselor.

Protect Yourself First
Remember, don't give others what you need the most yourself. Don't put masks on others when you haven't healed your own face yet. If you lose yourself, you can't help anyone else. Take care of your mind and heart first.

If you feel unsupported, write down your feelings in a journal. Practice breathing and meditation to stay calm, even when things are tough. Staying centered is your secret power.

Building Your Reputation Quietly and Steadily
You don't need to tell everyone your life story. Sometimes, friends and family get jealous — even without realizing it. When you succeed, it forces people to face themselves, and that can make them uncomfortable or even turn against you.

So protect your reputation. Be good to yourself. See yourself as the person you want to become — a millionaire, a leader, a creative genius. Your daily choices need to match that vision. If you say you want something, back it up with action and discipline.

Make specific plans — with dates and times — but don't stress about the "how." Focus on consistency. One day at a time. You don't have to read a million books, just the ones that matter.

Take control of your life. Be accountable. Know

when you're right and when you're wrong. Don't be quick to apologize, but when you are wrong, say sorry — and then move on. Don't keep apologizing to someone who won't listen.

Keep Your Dignity and Integrity

Set your own rules — your personal constitution — based on your values and morals. Don't wait for others to tell you what's right. Work hard and smart. Learn the rules of life — not necessarily to follow them blindly but to navigate and avoid unnecessary traps.

Keep your reputation squeaky clean. Keep your secrets close and only share what your intuition allows. Don't give people ammo to use against you when things get tough.

Master the Art of Asking Questions

When someone asks you too many personal questions, ask them back why they're interested or what they want to know. Then throw a deeper question at them — something they can't fake. Do it smoothly and confidently.

Practice this skill so when someone tries to catch you off guard, you're ready with a clever response. It's classy, powerful, and shows you're in control.

Example
Marcus always helps his family but knows when to say no. When his mom tried to ask too much, he calmly explained what he could handle. He also keeps his personal struggles private and only shares with a trusted cousin. Marcus is focused on school and his music, building his reputation quietly and steadily.

Message
You can be valuable and needed without losing yourself. Setting boundaries and protecting your energy is a sign of true strength.

Reflection
Think about times you've said "yes" when you really wanted to say "no." How did that affect you? What boundaries would you like to set now?

Journal Entry
Write about your values and limits. What are three

things you will say "no" to in order to protect your peace?

Questions to Ask Yourself
- How can I help others without burning out?
- What does "being needed" mean to me?

Questions to Ask Your Parents (when safe)
- What do you need from me right now?
- How can we support each other better?

Principles to Build
- Your energy is valuable — protect it.
- Boundaries are necessary, even with family.
- Reputation grows quietly, not through boasting.
- Accountability and consistency create success.
- Asking questions can be a powerful way to protect yourself.

Aha Moment
You realize that saying "no" and protecting your energy doesn't make you selfish — it makes you strong and respected.

Affirmations

- I am worthy of respect and kindness — especially from myself.
- I set boundaries that protect my peace and power.
- My reputation is built on honesty, discipline, and integrity.
- I am focused and consistent in building my future.
- I am confident in standing up for myself with grace.

Chapter 5:
The Power of Charisma and Emotional Intelligence — Master Them Like Your Life Depends On It

What Charisma Really Means for Teens

Charisma isn't just about being popular or having a flashy personality. It's about having a special kind of charm that draws people to you naturally. My own teen put it simply: "It's having enough charm to sway people." But there's more to it — charisma is about being real, relatable, and someone others want to be around because you make them feel understood and respected.

Simple Ways to Build Connection, Trust, and Respect

Charisma grows when you practice kindness, consideration, and wisdom. Speak less, listen more. Really listen. Show empathy and compassion — even if you haven't lived through the exact situation someone else is going through. Meet people where they are without judging them. When you make others feel safe and heard, they naturally want to be around you.

How Charisma Can Be Your Shield and Your Key

With charisma, people will fight for you, cover for you, and show up for you. It's like having a protective shield and a master key that opens doors. But charisma isn't something you're just born with — it's a skill you can learn and practice. Study it at your own pace. Don't overwhelm yourself with trying to be perfect. Start small and grow your influence naturally.

Why Emotional Intelligence Matters

Emotional intelligence — or EQ (Emotional Quotient) — is your ability to understand your own feelings and the feelings of others, and to respond thoughtfully. It's just as important as charisma. When you manage your emotions well, you avoid unnecessary conflicts and build stronger relationships. Being emotionally intelligent means you can stay calm under pressure, empathize with others, and make smart choices.

Tips to Grow Your Emotional Intelligence

- Notice how you feel in different situations — name your emotions.

- Practice calming techniques like deep breathing or counting to ten before reacting.
- Try to see things from other people's points of view.
- Reflect on your reactions and think about how you can improve next time.

Example

Jasmine isn't the loudest person in her group, but she listens well and always remembers what her friends say. When someone is upset, she knows how to calm them and offer support. Her classmates trust her and come to her for advice. That's charisma and emotional intelligence in action.

Message

Charisma and emotional intelligence aren't just "nice to have" — they're life tools. Master them and watch how your world opens up.

Reflection

Think about someone you admire for their personality or how they treat others. What do they do that makes people want to be around them?

How can you start practicing those traits?

Journal Entry
Write about a time you felt truly heard or understood. How did that affect you? What can you do to make others feel that way?

Questions to Ask Yourself
- How well do I listen to others?
- How do I handle my emotions when I'm upset or frustrated?

Questions to Ask Your Parents (when safe)
- How did you learn to manage your emotions growing up?
- What does being a good communicator mean to you?

Principles to Build
- Kindness and empathy build real connections.
- Listening is more powerful than talking.
- Emotional intelligence helps you stay calm and clear.
- Charisma is a skill you can grow, not just something you're born with.

Aha Moment

You realize that people are drawn not just to how you look or what you say, but how you make them feel — and that's a power you can develop.

Affirmations
- I am kind, considerate, and a good listener.
- I understand my emotions and use them wisely.
- I build trust and respect through empathy and honesty.
- My charisma grows every day as I practice being my true self.
- I attract positive and supportive people into my life.

Chapter 6:
Protecting Your Mental and Emotional Health — Preserve Your Energy Like Your Life Depends On It

Preserve Your Energy
Your mental and emotional health are precious. Don't waste your energy on excuses or trying to please everyone. Instead of saying "yes" when you really mean "no," give a raincheck — a polite way to say "not now." Avoid people, places, and activities that drain you, no matter what fancy name or title they have. Protect your vibe like it's gold, because it is.

Setting Invisible Boundaries with Toxic Parents
Know your ground and stand firm. Your safety is the priority. Learn to read the room — some parents might be unpredictable or more out of control than others. Know when to say what, and when it's better to stay silent. Invisible boundaries aren't about fighting — they're about protecting your peace without starting drama.

Finding Safe Spaces and People to Talk To
Create safe spaces for yourself — whether the

world feels calm or chaotic. Find people who genuinely want to see you succeed. But remember, no one is perfect. People make mistakes and sometimes disappoint. So be alert and protective. Always be the first and last person you speak to each day — trust yourself most of all.

Before you share your deepest thoughts, let people earn the right to hear them. Even when you feel alone, be patient with yourself. You're your own best friend.

Techniques to Stay Calm and Centered During Conflict

Practice being meditative — this means staying calm, aware, and focused even when things get tough. Always remember to breathe deeply and listen more than you speak. Try mindfulness techniques that work for you — journaling, meditation, yoga, mudras, walking, automatic writing — find your rhythm.

Avoid running to negative habits like drinking, drugs, or risky behavior, even "just for fun." Those quick escapes can trap you deeper when you're stressed. Instead, keep yourself "squeaky clean" — mentally, emotionally, and physically — so you preserve your energy and power.

When you feel triggered or gaslighted, don't sink. Transmute that energy — lift yourself higher. You have the power to rise above negativity and protect your peace.

Example
Tariq knows his dad can get angry suddenly. When tension rises, Tariq takes a few deep breaths and steps away to write in his journal. He doesn't engage in shouting matches. Instead, he waits for a calm moment to speak clearly and respectfully. This helps keep their fights from spiraling.

Message
Protecting your mental and emotional health is not selfish — it's survival. You are your own first line of defense.

Reflection
Think about a time when you felt emotionally drained after being around someone or something.

What could you have done differently to protect your energy?

Journal Entry

Write about your personal safe spaces — places, people, or activities that help you feel calm and strong. How can you spend more time in those spaces?

Questions to Ask Yourself
- What situations or people drain my energy?
- How can I create boundaries to protect myself?

Questions to Ask Your Parents (when safe)
- How do you handle stress and protect your peace?
- What can we do together to make home a calmer place?

Principles to Build
- Your energy is your most valuable resource — guard it.
- Invisible boundaries protect your peace without causing drama.

- Trust yourself above all — you are your best ally.
- Healthy coping skills are better than quick fixes.
- Transmute negativity by rising above it.

Aha Moment

You realize that mental and emotional health is about daily choices — how you protect your peace, what you say yes or no to, and how you manage your reactions.

Affirmations

- I protect my energy and peace with clear boundaries.
- I trust myself to stay calm and centered in any situation.
- I choose healthy habits that nourish my mind and body.
- I am my own strongest supporter and safest place.
- I rise above negativity and keep my light shining.

Chapter 7:
Black Sheep and Beyond — How to Shine When You're Ignored or Blamed

It's All About What You Allow and Accept

Being labeled the "black sheep" isn't a curse — it's about the meanings you accept and give to it. Your subconscious mind is powerful. If you change your beliefs about yourself, you change your reality. What others try to use as a weapon against you can become your secret power.

Why Being the Black Sheep Can Be Your Secret Power

Sure, being the outsider feels lonely and unfair. But that energy — the feeling of being different or ignored — can fuel your drive to succeed. When they think they're draining you, you're actually charging up. It becomes your reason to rise higher, to prove to yourself that you are unstoppable.

Stories of Teens Who Thrived Despite Rejection
- Maya's Story: Maya was always the quiet one in her family, often blamed when things went wrong. But instead of breaking down, she threw herself into art and music. Over time,

- Maya's talent blossomed, and she started sharing her work online. People loved her unique style, and soon she was invited to local exhibitions. Being the "black sheep" gave her the creative freedom to shine on her own terms.
- Jordan's Story: Jordan's parents never believed in his dream to become an athlete. They favored his older brother, who was the "golden child." Jordan faced criticism but kept training quietly. His persistence paid off when he earned a scholarship to a sports academy. Jordan's secret was resilience — he didn't let others' doubts define his future.

Cultivating Resilience and Self-Love

Resilience is your armor — it keeps you standing when the world tries to knock you down. But resilience alone isn't enough; you also need self-love. Love yourself fiercely, especially when others try to convince you that you're not lovable. Your worth isn't up for debate — it's unconditional and non-negotiable.

Building self-love means speaking kindly to yourself, celebrating your wins, and forgiving your mistakes. Remember, you are your longest commitment.

Example

When Noah's family ignored his successes and focused on his mistakes, he felt invisible. Instead of shrinking, Noah started a journal where he wrote down his daily wins and goals. That practice helped him build confidence and self-love, turning his black sheep label into a badge of honor.

Message

Your power grows when you decide not to let rejection define you. Being different can be your greatest strength.

Reflection

Think about a time you felt blamed or ignored. How did it make you feel? What can you learn from that experience to help you grow?

Journal Entry

Write a letter to your "black sheep" self — the part

that feels left out or misunderstood. What does that part need to hear right now?

Questions to Ask Yourself
- How do I turn negative energy into motivation?
- What are three things I love about myself?

Questions to Ask Your Parents (when safe)
- Can we talk about how I feel when I'm ignored or blamed?
- What do you see as my strengths?

Principles to Build
- Your labels don't define you — your actions do.
- Resilience and self-love are your greatest powers.
- Being different is a gift, not a weakness.
- Your story is yours to write — and rewrite.

Aha Moment
You realize that being the black sheep isn't a burden — it's your unique power waiting to be unleashed.

Affirmations

- I am powerful beyond what others see.
- I love and accept myself fully.
- I turn rejection into strength and success.
- My uniqueness is my greatest gift.
- I am worthy of love and belonging just as I am.

Chapter 8:
How to Get Help When You Need It — Be
Resourceful and Fearless

Help Yourself First

You are your greatest resource. If you need help,
go get it — but remember, no one can save you like
you can save yourself. Know who you are, and
you'll see that most things don't control you. You
have infinite power to manifest the life you want.
(That's a whole other chapter, but get familiar with
the idea!)

Always put yourself first — your safety, your peace,
your growth — above every situation.

Trusted Adults, Counselors, Hotlines, and Resources
There are people and places that can help —
teachers, counselors, hotlines, community groups.
But don't expect them to have all the answers.

They're human, with limits and flaws. Some are just
there for the paycheck, not because they care
deeply.

Before you open up, make sure the person is trustworthy. You can tell if someone respects themselves and others, no matter their age or status. Some adults only respect kids from "high status" families — don't be fooled by that. You deserve respect no matter what.

If someone disrespects or mocks you — step away. Trust your gut feelings; they are your safest guide. Your respect is a banner of safety. Imagine an adult who makes fun of you — what message does that send to others? Don't let anyone treat you like you don't matter.

When you need help, make sure people earn the right to hear your story. Sharing your truth is a privilege you give — don't give it away lightly. Bow to no one.

When and How to Ask for Help Without Fear
Be respectful and clear — you don't owe anyone proof or excuses. Stay powerful even while asking. Know how people think so you don't get played. Know your own gravity — your worth and presence.Asking for help doesn't make you weak or

less. It makes you wise — if you believe it. Own the space you occupy. Don't beg. Let your presence speak louder than your words. Believe in yourself.

Planning for Independence and Your Future
Your future and independence are your birthright. Don't be intimidated or scared. Don't erase yourself to fit in or to please others. Don't wait for permission to be powerful. The world only treats you as you allow it.

Speak like your words matter — because they do. You don't have to yell or shout. Power can be a quiet storm — a calm, steady force that people can't ignore or control.

Example
Sasha felt alone when her school counselor seemed uninterested. Instead of giving up, she found a youth support group online and started reading self-help books. She learned to trust her instincts and only shared her story with people who earned her trust. Sasha planned small steps toward college and a job, knowing her independence was hers to claim.

Message

Help is out there, but your first and best help is always from within. Trust yourself, be clear, and don't settle for less than respect.

Reflection

Think about a time when you needed help but felt scared or unsure. What stopped you? How could you approach it differently now?

Journal Entry

Write about who you trust most and why. What qualities do they have? How can you find or build more safe spaces and trusted people in your life?

Questions to Ask Yourself

- What does respect look like to me when asking for help?
- How can I prepare myself mentally before seeking support?

Questions to Ask Your Parents (when safe)

- Who do you trust to talk to when you need help?

- What advice do you have about asking for help and staying independent?

Principles to Build
- You are your own best resource — trust yourself first.
- Respect is non-negotiable, even when you're vulnerable.
- Asking for help is a sign of strength, not weakness.
- Your future is yours to claim — don't wait for permission.
- Quiet confidence is more powerful than loud demands.

Aha Moment
You realize that the power to get help and create your future starts with your belief in yourself and your willingness to stand firm in your worth.

Affirmations
- I am my greatest source of help and strength.
- I deserve respect no matter what I'm going through.

- Asking for help shows my courage and wisdom.
- I am the author of my future and my independence.
- My words carry power, even in silence.

Chapter 9:
Conclusion — Your Life Is Bigger Than Your Home

You Are a Force to Be Reckoned With

Don't ever let anyone make you feel small or powerless. You carry a strength inside that's unstoppable — even if it doesn't feel that way right now. Your life is bigger than your home, bigger than the drama or the unfairness. You are meant for greatness.

Encouragement for the Journey Ahead

Stay encouraged, but remember: the most important encouragement comes from you. No one is coming to save you — not because they can't, but because your mindset is your first line of defense. Believe you've got this. When help comes, it's a bonus — but you're the one who moves forward.

Affirmations for Self-Worth and Growth

Say these affirmations daily, especially during quiet moments or meditation. Don't just say them out loud; believe them. You're not only speaking words — you're working with invisible portals that open doors to your better self. Choosing to be better is a powerful decision.

Call to Action: Start Building Your Life Your Way
Have an unbreakable mind. Don't apologize for being powerful and strong. Stand tall, even when you feel pain or doubt — those feelings are illusions, and you control how much power you give them.

Start building your life now — don't wait for adulthood when responsibilities pile up. Sell to your friends, hire your siblings or cousins, start small and smart. Your teen years fly by fast, so be kind to yourself and focus on your own growth.

Remember: everyone else is busy focusing on themselves, even if they don't show it. I remember in my teens, I went out of my way for friends who were focused on themselves when it came to me. Don't burn out trying to be everything for everyone. Quietly focus on yourself. Build your empire one brick at a time. Your future self will thank you.

Example

Tania used to feel stuck at home, invisible and unheard. But she started setting small goals — selling handmade jewelry to friends, helping out at a local shop, and learning new skills online. Over time, she built confidence and independence quietly. Now, she's on her way to college with a plan — and her family sees her in a new light.

Message

Your journey is yours alone. No matter where you start, your future is full of possibilities. Believe in your power to shape it.

Reflection

What small steps can you take today toward building your future? How will focusing on yourself change your life?

Journal Entry

Write a letter to your future self. What do you want to remind yourself when things get hard? What goals do you want to celebrate?

Questions to Ask Yourself

- What does success look like to me?
- How can I protect my energy while working toward my dreams?
- Questions to Ask Your Parents (when safe)
- What were your dreams when you were my age?
- How did you overcome challenges growing up?

Principles to Build
- Your mindset is your most powerful tool.
- Growth is a daily, quiet process — not always loud or visible.
- Focusing on yourself is not selfish; it's necessary.
- Your future depends on the actions you take now.

Aha Moment
You realize that your power isn't waiting for permission — it's inside you now, ready to be used.

Affirmations
- I am powerful beyond measure.
- I stand tall no matter the challenges.
- My future is bright because I build it every day.

- I deserve success and happiness.
- I focus on my growth and trust my journey.

Chapter 10:
Start Building Your Empire Now — While You Still Can

You might think building your future is something you do after school, after college, or after life gets "serious." But here's a truth most grown-ups forget to tell you: The best time to start is now. While you still have the freedom to explore, dream, and even make mistakes without major responsibilities, you have a golden opportunity to plant seeds for your empire.

What Does Building Your Empire Mean?
It's not just about money or fame. It's about creating your own foundation — your skills, your confidence, your network, and your mindset — so when life throws challenges your way, you're ready. It's about owning your story and crafting the life you want on your own terms.

You don't have to have everything figured out. You don't need permission or special resources to start.

Use your time now to:
- Discover your talents and interests

- Learn new skills — even online for free
- Build relationships with people who lift you up
- Save small amounts of money, even if it's just a little
- Practice discipline and habits that support your goals

And yes — have fun with your friends, laugh, make memories. That's part of your foundation too. You don't need to sacrifice your joy to build your empire. In fact, joy and connection are your fuel.

Remember: *Your empire starts with you, right where you are.*

Example
Sammy loved basketball but never thought it could be more than a hobby. He started practicing daily, watching tutorials online, and joining local games. At the same time, he saved a bit of his allowance each week. Over time, his skills grew and he found new friends who shared his passion. Sammy's empire was growing — one step at a time.

Message

You don't need permission to start building your dreams. The best time to begin is always now.

Reflection

What talents or interests do I want to explore more? What small steps can I take today toward my goals?

Journal Entry

Write about a dream you have and what one thing you can do this week to move closer to it. How will you stay motivated?

Questions to Ask Yourself

- What am I passionate about?
- Who in my life supports and inspires me?

Principles to Build

- Start now — don't wait for the "right" time.
- Building your empire is about foundation, not speed.
- Joy and connection fuel your success.
- Discipline and consistency matter more than perfection.

Aha Moment

You realize that your future isn't something far away — it's built by the choices you make every day, starting right now.

Affirmations

- I am the builder of my own empire.
- Every small step I take creates my future.
- I deserve joy and success in my life.
- I am disciplined, focused, and unstoppable.
- My dreams are valid, and I will bring them to life.

Chapter 11:

Count on Nobody but Yourself — Your Ultimate Power

This might sound harsh, but it's one of the most important truths you need to know: People can disappoint you. Sometimes they don't mean to. Sometimes they don't even realize it. But sometimes, no matter how much you hope, they just won't come through.

That doesn't mean everyone will betray you — but it means you have to be prepared just in case. The key to staying strong and unshakable is this: Count on yourself first, and always.

When you rely on yourself, no one can let you down. You become your own protector, your own provider, your own greatest champion. You take full responsibility for your life — and that means you get to choose how you respond, what you build, and who you let in.

This doesn't mean you don't trust or love others. It means you put yourself first in a way that keeps you safe and empowered.

Here's how to start:
- Make promises to yourself — and keep them.
- Develop habits that build your strength and confidence.
- Learn to solve problems on your own first — then ask for help when you truly need it, but don't depend fully on anyone else.
- Practice saying "no" to people and things that don't serve you.
- Celebrate every win, no matter how small.

You are the foundation of your future. When you stand firm on yourself, nothing or no one can shake your peace or your power.

Example
Nia used to rely heavily on her friends to solve problems. When they weren't around, she felt lost and lonely. After learning to trust herself and handle things independently, Nia found new confidence. She still asks for help when needed but knows she's her own strongest supporter.

Message

Your power comes from within. Rely on yourself first — that's how you stay unbreakable.

Reflection

Think about a time when someone let you down. How did you handle it? How might relying more on yourself change things?

Journal Entry

Write about promises you want to make to yourself. What habits will help you keep them? How will you celebrate your progress?

Questions to Ask Yourself

- When have I solved a problem on my own and felt proud?
- What boundaries do I need to set to protect my peace?

Questions to Ask Your Parents (when safe)

- How did you learn to rely on yourself growing up?
- What advice do you have for standing strong through disappointment?

Principles to Build
- Self-reliance is your ultimate power.
- Boundaries protect your energy and peace.
- Asking for help is smart — depending on others completely is risky.
- Celebrating small wins builds confidence.
- You control your response and your future.

Aha Moment

You realize that the most dependable person in your life is you — and that gives you unstoppable power.

Affirmations
- I trust myself to handle life's challenges.
- I am my own strongest supporter and protector.
- I set clear boundaries to guard my peace.
- I celebrate every win, big or small.
- My power comes from within, and it is unshakable.

Bonus Chapter: Save Yourself (Reminder)

This might be one of the most important messages you'll ever receive — because your life, your future, and your spirit depend on it.

First, as a child or teen, DO NOT rush to have a child.

Enjoy your youth. Explore, learn, make mistakes — but don't let anyone pressure you into giving away your power before you're ready. Every time you lie down with someone, you share their energy, their karma, their family story — whether you realize it or not. What if that person's family has a history of pain, violence, or curses? Without your willing knowledge, you could be carrying burdens that aren't yours. Stay wise. Protect your energy.

Never let adults touch you in ways that feel wrong or uncomfortable.

This is manipulation. They are stealing your energy and dimming your light. This kind of harm sticks around longer than you might think — even if you learn to heal later. You don't have to curse those adults, but if they violate you, you have every right to protect yourself — spiritually and physically. Pray for trustworthy adults to guide you, but trust yourself first. Your gut is your best guardian — if it says run, then run.

Respect your parents no matter what.
You don't have to agree with everything they say or do, but don't disrespect, shame, humiliate, or curse them. They hold a sacred connection to you — your umbilical cord, your life, your ancestral lineage. That connection carries spiritual weight. We won't get too deep here, but it's enough to say: guard your words and actions toward them, even when the relationship is hard.

Don't get involved with married people.
This might sound old-fashioned, but it's true — relationships with married people carry hidden curses. They come with complex karma and alliances you don't want. You become marked and blocked from blessings. They're a team that may turn against you later. Protect your peace and your future by choosing wisely.

Give yourself strong life principles to avoid traps.
Negative forces want to trap you in cycles of pain,

betrayal, and limitation. But you have more power than you realize. Your ancestors are waiting on you to rise up, correct what's broken, protect your line, and break generational curses.

You are the one.
You have the strength, wisdom, and light to heal yourself and your family legacy. Honor that power. Save yourself — body, mind, and spirit.

Example
Jade was pressured by friends to rush into a relationship, but she chose to wait and focus on her goals. When she trusted her instincts and protected her energy, she avoided harmful situations and grew stronger. Jade's self-respect became her greatest shield.

Message
Your life and spirit are sacred. Protect them fiercely by making wise choices and trusting yourself.

Reflection
Think about a time when you ignored your gut or

felt pressured. What happened? How can you honor your intuition better going forward?

Journal Entry

Write a letter to your younger self with advice on protecting your energy and respecting your worth. What would you say?

Questions to Ask Yourself
- How do I recognize when my boundaries are being crossed?
- Who are the trustworthy adults in my life I can turn to?

Principles to Build
- Your energy and spirit are sacred — protect them.
- Trust your intuition — it's your best guide.
- Boundaries are necessary for your safety and growth.
- Self-respect is your strongest shield.
- You have ancestral power supporting your healing and growth.

Aha Moment

You realize that saving yourself isn't selfish — it's your sacred duty to your future and your family legacy.

Affirmations

- I honor and protect my energy and spirit.
- I trust my intuition and listen to my inner voice.
- I am worthy of respect and love.
- I set clear boundaries to guard my peace.
- I am powerful and supported by my ancestors.

Here we want to share more affirmations, practical exercises, and spiritual wisdom tailored for you to pair with your powerful Bonus Chapter "Save Yourself." This will help you internalize the message, protect your energy, and connect deeper with your spirit.

Affirmations for Protecting Your Energy and Spirit

- I am a sacred vessel, and I protect my energy with love and strength.
- My intuition is a powerful guide that always leads me to safety.
- I deserve relationships and spaces that honor and uplift me.
- I release what no longer serves me and welcome healing and peace.
- I am connected to my ancestors and their strength flows through me.
- I set boundaries with confidence, knowing they keep me whole.
- Every day, I grow stronger in mind, body, and spirit.
- I am worthy of love, respect, and divine protection.

Practical Exercises to Strengthen Your Spirit and Protect Your Energy

1. Daily Energy Check-In

Take 5 minutes each day to sit quietly and check in with your energy. Close your eyes and ask:

- How do I feel right now?
- What thoughts or feelings are weighing on me?
- What can I do to protect or restore my energy today?
- Write down your answers and make a plan to care for yourself.

2. The Sacred Boundary Circle

Imagine drawing a glowing circle of light around yourself — your sacred boundary. Visualize it as strong and impenetrable, only allowing positive energy and people you trust inside. Whenever you feel overwhelmed or unsafe, mentally reinforce this circle.

3. Journaling Your Intuition

Each day, write about moments when your gut told you something important. Reflect on how you acted and what you learned. This practice builds trust in your inner voice.

4. Ancestral Connection Meditation

Find a quiet space and sit comfortably. Close your eyes and breathe deeply. Visualize a warm, glowing light above your head — your ancestors' energy flowing into you, filling you with strength, wisdom, and protection. Repeat silently or aloud:

"I am guided and protected by the strength of those who came before me."

Spend 5-10 minutes in this meditation whenever you feel disconnected or weak.

5. Releasing Negative Energy Ritual

When you feel drained or weighed down, try this simple ritual:

- Write down on paper what is troubling you or draining your energy.
- Safely burn the paper (or tear it up and throw it away) while saying:
- "I release all negativity that no longer serves me. I am free, whole, and healed."
- This symbolic act helps you let go and reclaim your power.

Spiritual Wisdom for Teens

Your Spirit is Eternal and Powerful

Even when your body feels tired or your mind is overwhelmed, your spirit is an unbreakable flame. It carries the wisdom and strength of generations before you — your ancestors who survived, thrived, and protect you now. You are never alone.

Your Boundaries Are Sacred

Setting boundaries is not about pushing people away — it's about creating space for your light to shine. When you honor yourself with boundaries, you invite respect and positive energy into your life.

Trust Your Inner Compass

Your intuition is a divine gift. It's your internal GPS, guiding you through challenges, helping you avoid danger, and leading you toward growth. Practice listening to it daily, even in small decisions.

Healing is Your Birthright

No matter what you've experienced or inherited, healing is possible. It starts with awareness and a commitment to nurture yourself — mind, body, and spirit. Every step you take toward healing is a victory.

You Are the Bridge Between Past and Future
You carry ancestral wisdom and have the power to break cycles of pain and limitation. Your choices today ripple forward to heal not only your life but your family's lineage. Walk this path with courage and grace.

Final Wrap-Up & Guide:
How to Use This Book to Transform Your Life

Congratulations on completing this journey — you've gathered powerful tools, truths, and wisdom to help you survive and thrive, no matter what your home looks like.

But reading is just the first step. The magic happens when you use what you've learned every day. Here's how to get the most from this book and create real change:

1. Take It One Chapter at a Time
Don't rush. Each chapter is a seed planted for your growth. Read it slowly. Reflect deeply. Use the reflection questions and journal prompts to understand yourself better and plan your next steps.

2. Create Your Own Healing Routine
Pick one or two affirmations from each chapter to say daily. Try at least one practical exercise regularly — whether it's setting boundaries, practicing mindfulness, or building your empire.

Small consistent actions add up to big transformations.

3. Use Your Journal as Your Safe Space
Your journal is your best friend. Use it to be honest, process feelings, celebrate wins, and plan your future. Return to it whenever you feel lost or overwhelmed. Writing helps you heal and stay grounded.

4. Trust Your Inner Wisdom
You have all the answers inside you. Use the tools in this book to connect with your intuition. When faced with challenges, pause, breathe, and ask yourself: "What does my heart say?" Your gut will never steer you wrong.

5. Set Boundaries and Protect Your Energy
Remember: Your peace is sacred. Use the boundaries strategies to keep toxic energy out. It's okay to say no, walk away, or ask for space. You are your first priority.

6. Build Your Support System Carefully
Reach out to trusted adults, friends, or counselors

— but only those who respect and uplift you. Let people earn the privilege to be part of your story. You decide who deserves your time and energy.

7. Celebrate Your Progress

Every step forward — no matter how small — is a victory. Celebrate your courage, your growth, and your resilience. You are rewriting your story and creating your legacy.

8. Remember Your Power and Purpose

You are the author of your life. Your family history doesn't define you; your choices do. You have ancestral strength backing you. Stand tall, shine bright, and walk your path with confidence.

Final Affirmations to Carry Forward

- I am worthy of love, respect, and happiness.
- I am the master of my story and the builder of my future.
- My peace and energy are sacred and protected.
- I trust myself to make wise choices every day.
- I am powerful, resilient, and unstoppable.

We want you to know that:
- Your life is your greatest project. Use this book as your guide, your shield, and your launchpad. Come back to it whenever you need strength or clarity.
- You've got this, always.

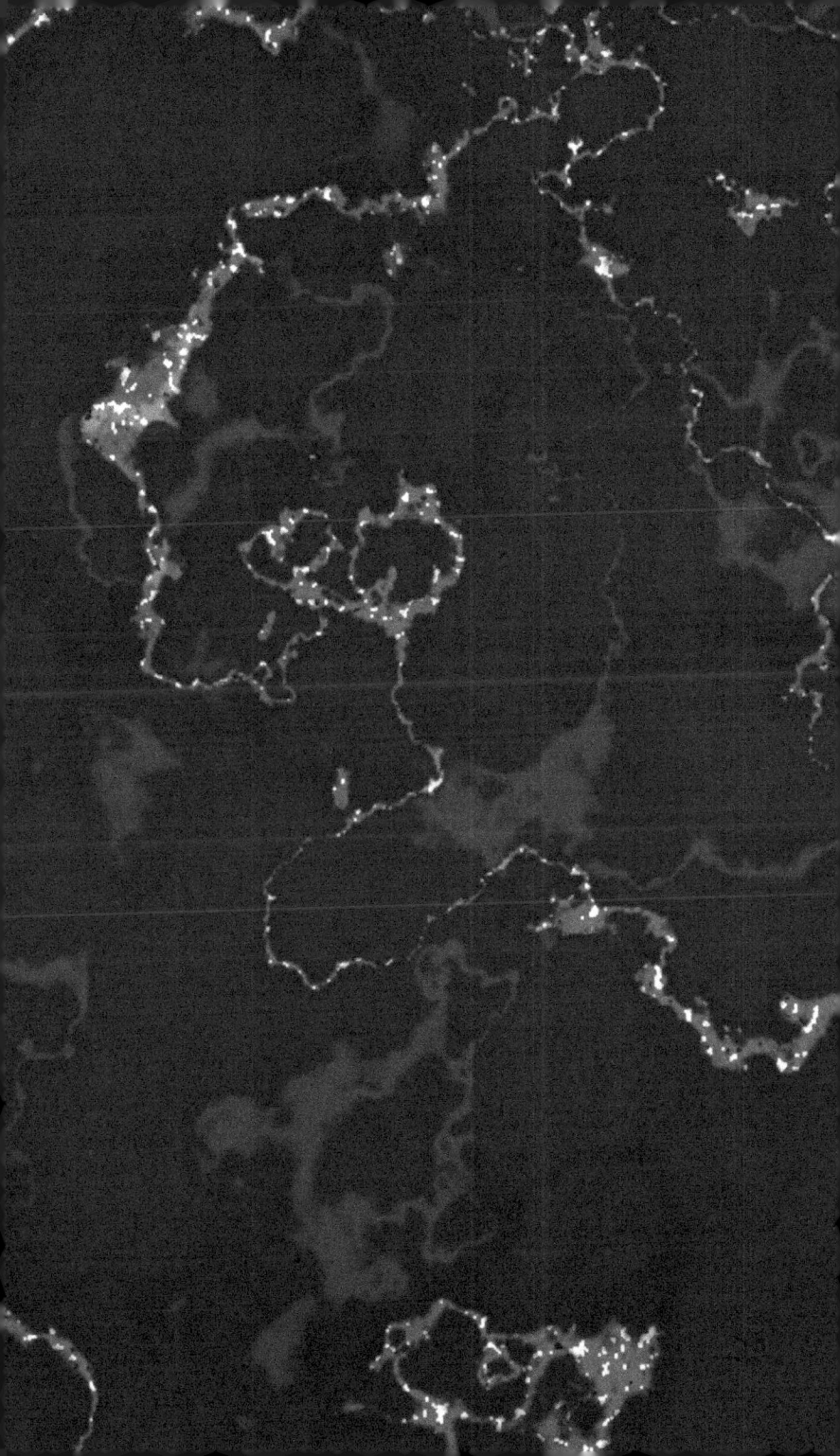

Your Personal Growth Tracker & Planner (because you have to read this again with a brand new intention, and you can make copies or take a picture to keep up and monitor yourself)

Weekly Check-In:
- Chapter I'm focusing on this week:

  _____
  _____
  _____

- One new habit I'm practicing:

  _____
  _____
  _____

- Affirmation I'm repeating daily:

  _____
  _____
  _____

- Challenge I faced this week:

  _____
  _____
  _____

- How I handled it:

  _____

  _____

  _____

- One thing I'm proud of:

  _____

  _____

  _____

- What I want to improve next week:

  _____

  _____

  _____

Monthly Reflection (Similar to above, this is to plan, keep track, evaluate, monitor, etc...)

- What was my biggest breakthrough this month?

  _____

  _____

  _____

- What habits became easier or stronger?

  _____

  _____

  _____

- How did I protect my energy this month?

  _____

  _____

  _____

- Who supported me and how?

  _____

  _____

  _____

What's one new goal I want to set for next month?

_____

_____

_____

_____

_____

Daily Quick Check

- How do I feel today?
- (Circle) Calm / Stressed / Happy / Sad / Other: _____
- Notes:

_____

_____

_____

- Did I say my affirmations? Yes / No

_____

_____

_____

- What's one positive thing I did today?

_____

_____

_____

What's one to three things I want to do better tomorrow? Why?

_____

_____

_____

_____

_____

_____

_____

_____

_____

_____

_____

_____

_____

_____

_____

_____

_____

This tracker can be printed, written in a notebook, or saved on your phone. Use it to keep yourself accountable and mindful of your growth.

Your Personal Growth Tracker & Planner (because you have to read this again with a brand new intention, and you can make copies or take a picture to keep up and monitor yourself)

Weekly Check-In:
- Chapter I'm focusing on this week:

_____
_____
_____

- One new habit I'm practicing:

_____
_____
_____

- Affirmation I'm repeating daily:

_____
_____
_____

- Challenge I faced this week:

_____
_____
_____

- How I handled it:

_____

_____

_____

- One thing I'm proud of:

_____

_____

_____

- What I want to improve next week:

_____

_____

_____

Monthly Reflection (Similar to above, this is to plan, keep track, evaluate, monitor, etc...)

- What was my biggest breakthrough this month?

  _____
  _____
  _____

- What habits became easier or stronger?

  _____
  _____
  _____

- How did I protect my energy this month?

  _____
  _____
  _____

- Who supported me and how?

  _____
  _____
  _____

What's one new goal I want to set for next month?

_____
_____
_____
_____
_____

Daily Quick Check
- How do I feel today?
- (Circle) Calm / Stressed / Happy / Sad / Other:_____
- Notes:_____

_____
_____
_____

- Did I say my affirmations? Yes / No

_____
_____
_____

- What's one positive thing I did today?

_____
_____
_____

What's one thing I want to do better tomorrow?

_____

_____

_____

_____

_____

_____

_____

_____

_____

_____

_____

_____

_____

_____

_____

_____

_____

_____

This tracker can be printed, written in a notebook, or saved on your phone. Use it to keep yourself accountable and mindful of your growth.

Notes.

_____

Notes.

_____
_____
_____
_____
_____
_____
_____
_____
_____
_____
_____
_____
_____
_____
_____
_____
_____
_____
_____
_____
_____

Notes.

_____

_____

_____

_____

_____

_____

_____

_____

_____

_____

_____

_____

_____

_____

_____

_____

_____

_____

_____

Notes.

_____
_____
_____
_____
_____
_____
_____
_____
_____
_____
_____
_____
_____
_____
_____
_____
_____
_____
_____
_____
_____

Notes.

_____
_____
_____
_____
_____
_____
_____
_____
_____
_____
_____
_____
_____
_____
_____
_____
_____
_____
_____
_____
_____

Notes.

_____
_____
_____
_____
_____
_____
_____
_____
_____
_____
_____
_____
_____
_____
_____
_____
_____
_____
_____
_____
_____

Notes.

Notes.

_____

_____

_____

_____

_____

_____

_____

_____

_____

_____

_____

_____

_____

_____

_____

_____

_____

_____

_____

_____

_____